Labyrinth Canyon River Guide

Green River, Utah

2005 Edition

Thomas G. Rampton

Blacktail Enterprises
Nathrop, Colorado

www.blacktail-enterprises.com

*Blacktail Canyon is tributary to
the Colorado River in Grand Canyon*

Labyrinth Canyon River Guide: Green River, Utah. Copyright © 2005 by Thomas G. Rampton. Printed and bound in the United States of America. All rights reserved. No part of this book may be reproduced in any form or by any electronic means including information storage and retrieval systems without permission in writing from the publisher, except by a reviewer, who may quote brief passages in a review. Published by Blacktail Enterprises, Nathrop, Colorado 81236.

Photographs are by Thomas G. Rampton. The **cover photo** is in the tight meanders of Labyrinth Canyon. The **aerial photographs** were all made on 7 April 2005 while flying with Trent Fluckey of Green River Aviation. **Editing** was by Evan Yamakawa of Tumwater, Washington. Considerable help with cover design came from Anrahyah Arstad and a color idea came from Damien Mayo.

Maps are from i-cubed in Fort Collins, Colorado. This company provides digital USGS 1:24000 topographic maps. River miles generally (though not exactly) follow those of Belknap, which are widely used.

This book was produced using Microsoft Windows and Word; Adobe Photoshop and InDesign—all of which are trademarks. The book exists as a computer file, from which it is printed on an offset book press.

Disclaimer: This guide sometimes suggests specific actions on the river, particularly at rapids. But no guide can replace your own judgement or compensate for your possible lack thereof. You must ultimately make your own decisions. Rivers, riverbanks, and rapids can change radically with water level, and over time. Launch areas and campsites change. Internet addresses and phone numbers change. Everything changes. Personal river running styles differ, and a written description is subject to interpretation. Neither this guide, nor any Internet updates or other information provided, can be warranted against possible error or omission.

Publisher's Cataloging-in-Publication *(Provided by Quality Books, Inc.)*

Rampton, Thomas G.
  Labyrinth Canyon river guide / Thomas G. Rampton. -- 2005 ed.
  p. cm.
  ISBN-13: 978-0-9634799-6-9
  ISBN-10: 0-9634799-6-2

  1. Rafting (Sports)--Green River (Wyo.-Utah)--Guidebooks. 2. Outdoor recreation--Labyrinth Canyon (Utah) 3. Green River (Wyo.-Utah)--Guidebooks. 4. Geology--Green River Vally (Wyo.-Utah) 5. Labyrinth Canyon (Utah)--Guidebooks.   I. Title.

GV776.G744R355 2005   797.1'21'097925
                    QBI05-600021

To those who love river canyons and work to protect their magnificence

Green River near Keg Spring Canyon

Table of Contents

Introduction	5
Green River to Mineral Bottom	7
River Access	21
Four Labyrinth Trips	27
Regional Geology	37
Area Map	47
Detailed Maps	48

Mouth of Three Canyon from west rim

Introduction

"There is an exquisite charm in our ride down this beautiful canyon. We are all in fine spirits. Now and then we whistle or shout or discharge a pistol, to listen to the reverberations among the cliffs. We name this Labyrinth Canyon."

Labyrinth Canyon isn't a whitewater trip, but note these words of river explorer John Wesley Powell. In 1869, he and his weary crew had just been through several whitewater stretches upstream. They found easy water and respite in this place of vertical, visual power.

We can still do that today. Labyrinth Canyon is on Utah's Green River between the town of that name on Interstate 70 and Mineral Bottom, 68 miles downstream. The confluence of the Green and the Colorado Rivers is another 52 miles down from Mineral Bottom. The next takeout is over a hundred miles away, though jet boat service up the Colorado is available.

Rapids exist here, but they are not intense. Except for The Auger near Crystal Geyser, they are within a mile of the launch at Green River State Park. The Auger is the largest and last rapid between Green River and Mineral Bottom. Thereafter, calm prevails all the way to Cataract Canyon, except for a riffle that's far downstream. Other swift spots and riffles do exist here or there at low water.

Labyrinth is a popular canoe trip. I've done it by inflatable kayak and raft. I've been to rim overlooks, and have flown the river. The canyon doesn't develop immediately beyond Green River. First, there are 25 miles where the river flows around bottomlands and under low bluffs.

There is extensive human history all along this part of the Green River, particularly on this first stretch. To learn more, read *River Guide to Canyonlands National Park and Vicinity* by Michael R. Kelsey.

Kelsey's book is meticulously researched, partly through interviews with old timers in the region. You will find that almost every one of these canyons and bottomlands involves a rich story and maybe a dastardly killing. Kelsey doesn't write about how to conduct a river trip, but about colorful characters and their difficult doings.

For those first 25 miles, the bluffs along the river will tease you by rising, then falling away. Several dirt roads reach the river, though you won't see many people unless at Crystal Geyser or Ruby. You'll float past the geyser, Little Valley, a gravel operation, some abandoned mine works, and Ruby Ranch. There is river access at Crystal Geyser, and a good boat ramp at Ruby, exactly opposite the mouth of the San Rafael River. See *River Access*.

Then you'll float into Labyrinth Canyon where sandstone walls will tower over you. The river has entrenched itself deeply. A series of tight meanders will be followed by a larger one at Bowknot Bend.

At http://water.usgs.gov/ut/nwis/current/?type=flow the relevant gauge for Labyrinth Canyon water level is station 09315000, "Green River at Green River, UT." This is the same gauge you'd check for Desolation Canyon upstream. Clicking on the station number shows you a graph of water levels for the preceding week. This can help you discern trends. In addition, the Colorado Basin River Forecast Center gives recorded flow information by phone at 810-539-1311.

The highest flow ever recorded was 68,100 cubic feet per second on 27 June 1917. The lowest was 255 cfs on 26 November 1931. Since I've been watching, the river rose to about 48,000 in June of 1984. But it stayed below 1,000 nearly all summer in 2002, following the driest of several consecutive semi-winters in the west.

A strong runoff should bring down perhaps 20,000 cfs in late May or early June. Even a weak runoff should give you half of that. In most years, you'll likely still have two or three thousand cubic feet per second by the end of the season. That's good floating.

High water may allow you to float into some camps that would be more difficult to reach at medium levels. Low water leaves sand bar camps all over the place. With a change in water level, you may see a difference in camp accessibility and width of the "mud zone. "

The trip will take longer at low water and you'll be finding your way around sand bars. But it's not as though there's a huge rapid down there that's unrunnable when the water is wrong! Water level doesn't make as much difference in Labyrinth as it may elsewhere. Personally, I'd like to make an autumn trip there sometime.

For further Bureau of Land Management information, see the rather complete website at www.blm.gov/utah/price or phone the BLM in Price at 435-636-3460 for the office, or 435-636-3622 for the river unit.

ATTENTION PLEASE! THIS WOULD BE A POOR THING TO FORGET. Over Memorial Day Weekend, the annual Friendship Cruise is held. Unless the water is too low, a multitude of power boats leave Green River, go downstream to the confluence, and up the Colorado to Moab. This would be an experience to watch or participate in, but not if you seek solitude in the canyon or even a camp. It's a cruise, not a race. The boats will take two or three days for the journey and they may stop anywhere. Check the site at http://ecso.com/friendship/index.html and plan accordingly.

Enjoy Labyrinth! Most often peaceful and primitive, it's yet another unique and wonderful portion of the Green River.

Green River to Mineral Bottom

120.0 Green River State Park in Green River, Utah is a fine place to camp and launch. You'll be on grass under large trees, and there's a paved launch ramp. The park is worth the fee. See *River Access*.

119.8 You'll go under the railroad bridge, which is immediately downstream and plainly visible from the state park launch ramp.

119.6 Where to go at the first island? More water appeared to go left but I couldn't see over there. The river dropped through a minor riffle on the right. It surely didn't matter, just as many things don't matter once you're on the water, but an overriding consideration arose: The right side afforded shade! We went right.

119.3 Interstate 70 (I-70) crosses the river here and there's a riffle under the bridge. Over the next few miles, a canyon begins gently. Low bluffs rise and the hills get higher downstream. The first sandstone appears and insects may scream in the tamarisk.

118.1 The river turns right. Evidence of a landslide is seen on the left.

117.5 Some sandstone layers on the left here are lenticular bodies. That means thick in the middle and thinning toward the edges like the cross section of a lens—just as we'd expect for deposition in stream channels. Dig through a present-day river sandbar, and you'll find the same shape.

The lenticular deposits here, if studied, give evidence of deposition by streams that flowed northward, unlike those today.

117.1 Camp on the right.

116.8 On the left there's a pump, a small orchard just visible over the shoreline vegetation, and a small green-colored house that appears to be occupied. Low bluffs continue on both sides.

115.4 Crystal Geyser is identified by orange material crystallized from water that has erupted. A large diameter pipe stands up out of a pool: The geyser is actually an abandoned well. There are wavy ripples on the surface of the orange deposits where travertine has been deposited. Evaporation of mineralized water occurs just a little faster on the lips of these ripples, so they grow. Small pools are here and there.

The geyser wasn't active when we approached in 2001, but the overall wetness made me hesitate to stand downwind with my camera. It erupted nicely during a later visit by land.

A camp is possible here, though trash was around when we looked. A common launch, Crystal Geyser is easily accessible from the town of Green River. See *River Access*.

The Little Grand Fault runs across the river just downstream of Crystal Geyser. The downstream side is downthrown, which means it moved in that direction relative to the other side.

A few words about private property between Green River and Ruby Ranch—much of the land is exactly that. But there are significant stretches of public land as well. Crystal Geyser is public, for example.

One bank may be private and the other public. The reverse may be true, or both banks may be one or the other. The pattern is rather complex along this upper portion of your trip.

A saving grace is this: According to Dennis Willis of the BLM office in Price, UT, you are free to camp anywhere provided you stay below the mean high water line, even where there is private land above you. You can also camp freely on bars and islands which are state land regardless of the high water mark. Islands often have camps at their heads or tails.

If the water is low these tips may prove useful, but at high water you may speed on down and not need a camp until you're past Ruby Ranch. I know camps change, so I'll only mark the most obvious and durable. I won't mark most sandbar camps because at high water there won't be any, and at low water they'll abound.

I differentiate between obvious camps that I show in yellow—and those that for some reason are not certain, may not be accessible, only exist at lower water, or are where land ownership is unclear because of nearness to a property line. These are shown in orange.

From nearly opposite the launch at Ruby Ranch, the right will be public the rest of the way. Land on the left from approximately mile 95.3 will also be public. The BLM publishes maps showing private and public land. The relevant one is named *San Rafael Desert, Utah*. Farther down, a tiny bit of river is on the *Moab, Utah* map. For four bucks each, the Price BLM office will mail maps to you.

114.9 The Auger, a minor rapid where, at lower water, the river divides into multiple channels of which the far right seemed best. There may be camps on island bars.

The country returns to more openness after The Auger. The river heads west for a couple of miles and you'll have an open vista straight ahead to the jagged eastern flank of the San Rafael Swell—which stands as a monument to Laramide uplift. There, sedimentary rock layers were bowed upward during the Laramide Orogeny and have since been eroded back so that only a jagged crest remains. See *Regional Geology*.

The Swell is a fruitful place to look for slot canyons. Michael Kelsey did, and wrote *Technical Slot Canyon Guide to the Colorado Plateau*.

Little Valley is the large bottomland on the left. It extends from about mile 114 past mile 111. Pumps and other machinery are in evidence here. A maintained road follows the left bank downstream from Crystal Geyser, but you will come to a locked gate.

112.9 There are two abandoned cabins and possibly a travel trailer on the right. A road goes out. This place looks private, and the map agrees.

112.3 Dark gray rock appears and forms the bluffs on the right. This is the Cretaceous-age Mancos Shale, here soft and thin-bedded with several layers of sandy sediment. Fallen bits make for a smooth talus slope extending from the cliffs down to the water.

Little Valley continues on the left. We noticed a truck and a large stack of hay bales there. The river finally turns south again, toward Labyrinth.

111.7 Camp on the right, but it's on private land.

111.5 View upriver to the top of the Book Cliffs, which mark the end of Gray Canyon. Farther away, also visible, are the Roan Cliffs which mark the end of Desolation Canyon near Three Fords Rapid.

Signs on the left bank command boaters to keep out. No matter the temptation, don't you dare trespass here! Just don't do it, even though this place is particularly scenic as gravel pits go.

111.0 There is a cabin on the right, near the mouth of Ninemile Wash. This form of the name, like "Twomile" far downstream, is supported by USGS topo maps. Access is from the Green River Road which goes south from that town and angles left off the airport road.

The canyon slowly begins to deepen again. The sedimentary rock layers are seen to "dip" gently upstream, which here means they slowly rise from the river and climb onto the cliffs ahead of you.

Small tributary canyons emerge from the low bluffs now and then with occasional thick-trunked cottonwoods. A tiny jet of swifter water may aid your progress as the river swirls mysteriously around hidden bars. You'll move along at a decent speed.

110.0 Sediments here are more massive; they're of chocolate-colored sandstone now. The bluffs are slowly growing higher.

109.6 Camp on the right, on state land.

109.1 You float along a wall of sandstone on the left where the rock has been undercut and worked by the river to be full of openings. The same rock a little higher isn't eroded in this way. You are near the first and north-most bounding fault of the Salt Wash Graben, where a block half a mile wide sank between two faults that cross the river.

The terrain has become more canyon-like, but open country begins again at mile 109. This transition between canyon and openness is repetitive. It's related to hard and soft layers of rock that slope up to the surface and also to the presence of faults, like this one. The happy trend is toward higher walls and greater isolation.

108.6 Here is the south-most bounding fault of the Salt Wash Graben.

107.8 A mine is on the right at McCarty Bottom where, according to the BLM, vehicles can reach the river.

107.1 Low water ledge camp on the right. The land here is public.

105.6 Possible camp, on public land near mouth of Salt Water Wash.

105.5 There are several places in this area where one could scratch out a camp. The land continues to be public on both sides, and will down through approximately mile 103.

105.2 Camp at the foot of an island.

101.9 There's a nice camp on the left, under and along a ledge (read: rain shelter), just before Anvil Bottom. It's at the foot of the prominence that includes Dellenbaugh's Butte. Frederick Dellenbaugh, at age 17, was the artist on Powell's second expedition. Locally, his butte is also called The Anvil, or The Inkwell.

It's difficult to tell from the BLM map whether this camp is on public land or not, but I believe it is by just a little. On some future trip I will use GPS to check this further, but for now I have marked this camp in yellow.

100.7 There's a row of pink sandstone cliffs on the left, and pinkish dunes on the right.

100.0 The left opens out into Entrada Sandstone slickrock.

99.0 Waterwheel on the left bank. Several of these were built to do useful work for their owners. One that didn't is mentioned in *Four Labyrinth Trips*. There's a large pipe, an old cabin, and a modern house here. Ruby Ranch property begins on the left.

97.2 Possible camp on the right—at or near a Powell camp. From here, one map shows a trail that runs above the San Rafael River to the Chaffin Ranch, from which a road goes 22 miles out to Green River.

I drove to the Chaffin Ranch from Green River in the spring of 2004. Nothing is left of it now except several deceased cars and a small geyser. Kelsey implies that water from this geyser is worse than unpotable. You are unlikely to learn firsthand from me whether or not this is true.

97.0 Ruby Ranch launch ramp (38°46.64'N 110°06.31'W). This is a pleasant area among trees, opposite the unimpressive mouth of the San Rafael River. We slept at Ruby once, and got off early. See *River Access*.

Ruby Ranch extends for about three miles along the left bank. Two water pumps turned by big motors operate nearby, irrigating the large field. Noise is inevitable but understandable.

96.2 There is mining machinery above the left bank here.

95.7 Camp right, where a trail goes up a steep bank. Serviceable, but far from great. It's just beyond the sound of the water pumps.

95.0 The river swings up against the Navajo Sandstone for the first time. Only the left bank will be Navajo for about a mile. After the river curves south again near mile 94, both banks will be of that Mesozoic sandstone.

The walls get higher as the rock slopes upward downstream and it seems that you're in the canyon at last. But no—the left soon opens out.

94.4 Camp on the left with a bar extending behind some big rocks. At medium water and above, this place would be awash.

Green River to Mineral Bottom 11

Dellenbaugh's Butte, mile 101

93.8 Now you're almost there! The Green River turns around the bottomland. Soon there's a view down a straight stretch where you'll see the river disappear into Labyrinth Canyon.

93.7 A prominent cliff of Navajo Sandstone continues on your right. A small fence is visible atop the Navajo there, just where a trail leaves the rim to angle down to the river at Bull Bottom. The fence just keeps livestock off the trail. I drove to the top here in 2004.

90.0 Three Canyon on the right (38°42.43'N 110°07.39'W) as the river curves around Trin Alcove Bend. This is a special place, said to be the last canyon of its type not destroyed by Powell Reservoir. There's a good landing, and a large camp about 50 yards up under a cliff of Navajo Sandstone. Other sleeping areas are down among the trees. The camps at Three Canyon are very well used, so I wouldn't plan to arrive there just before dark with no other options.

A well-used trail goes up the canyon. You'll soon come to flowing water, and can walk to a fine place where the cliff is undercut on the south-most side. Flowing water was pooled along the wall here. I'd been told about a wonderful spring-fed pool up Three Canyon and I believe I found it, but the water was very low.

Kelsey reports a great hike to the upper end of Three Canyon where there are fantastic narrows, a flowing stream, and impassable dry falls at the end. This is one of the better hikes in Labyrinth, he writes.

Powell first explored and named this place, noting that three tributary canyons join here. I have trouble counting much past two, though there is a much smaller reentrant near the confluence of the two major ones.

One time, we floated inflatable kayaks about 200 yards up the canyon to a great camp—but this was at very high water; about 30,000 cfs. You won't normally be able to do that. See *Four Labyrinth Trips*.

88.1 Camp on the left, of medium size. It has a steep bank, but at lower water there's a cooking area down by the river.

87.3 A nice camp on the left (38°42.39'N 110°05.14W) at the mouth of a small canyon. We camped here and explored up the very short tributary. At its head we found seeps in the rock and a small flow of water. See *Four Labyrinth Trips*.

We shared this camp in 2004 with a canoe group from Utah Valley State College. One of those students had participated in a Labyrinth Canyon canoe race that one professor would organize each spring. The story was about heavy meteorological hardship during the race just three months earlier. See *Four Labyrinth Trips*.

87.0 The Navajo Sandstone is underlain first by the Kayenta Formation and then by the Wingate Sandstone (which has not yet appeared). Together, these three are called the Glen Canyon Group. They're still rising downstream so the canyon will get deeper as you go. A few ledges up in the Kayenta Formation, on the left, there are several large holes in the rock that appear to interconnect.

86.5 On the left are two camps, with paths up onto rocky ledges that support the bottomland. The first camp has trees, but the second doesn't. If you're looking, stay left of a small island at lower water.

84.0 Camp on the left, at the far end of a long, sheer sandstone wall. There's a landing behind two fallen rocks that project into the river. This was a good camp for us one 10th of June, except we apparently hit that year's mosquito hatch. See *Four Labyrinth Trips*.

83.6 Long island left of center, with room at lower water for several groups to camp. Downstream, the island is higher and drier.

82.8 Petroglyphs are on the left, about where the bottomland ends.

82.1 Here is the first cliff of Wingate Sandstone. With towering vertical walls, the Wingate is in large part responsible for making Labyrinth Canyon what it is. Its appearance at river level is a good omen! The Wingate rises directly from the water here, and its base is undercut a little. The river may slap and burble against the rock.

For the next several miles, the Green will flow through a series of tight, symmetrical, entrenched meanders in the Wingate Sandstone. These continue until approximately Hey Joe Canyon near mile 76..

81.0 Small opening (38°39.47'N 110°04.35'W) through the tamarisk to a fine, large camp with trees on the upper portion of Ten Mile Bottom. Beyond, the bottom is open to the first slope of the canyon wall.

80.5 Camp on the left, at Tenmile Bottom immediately above the mouth of the wash. The camp is only about 20 yards upstream from the wash (38°39.54'N 110°03.88W), but we saw no way into it from the mouth except with great difficulty. So land in time!

For a long way after the wash, we heard what must have been wild turkeys clucking in the bushes as we floated along. Though one turkey may have been following us, it seems more likely that new ones took up the call as we floated by.

79.5 From here, the river appears at first to flow straight ahead, but it will turn left. What you see ahead is Keg Spring Canyon.

79.3 Camp on the left at the very beginning of a bottomland, with the first landing behind some projecting rocks. There is a second landing, and a third (38°39.24'N 110°03.42'W).

We thought this large camp was one of the best on the river. It's in the visible group of trees, and has a flat rock that can be used for a small table. This camp even has a king! He is a large lizard who rules from atop a sawed-off stump and does pushups. This is said to be lizard talk for "leave me alone!"

79.0 Keg Spring Canyon (38°38.87'N 110°03.53'W) on the right. We didn't land, but there looks to be a camp of some description there on the upstream side of the tributary. The satellite photos at maps.google.com were inconclusive. There's a trail out to the rim here, according to the BLM site.

77.5 River Register on the left, where boaters over the years (but not anymore, please) have added their names. Now, there is major concern about people scratching or scrawling stuff on the walls anywhere, not just here. Very near the register is a good landing. You are entering a small syncline, where the rock layers bend downward and then back up again.

75.8 Mouth of Hey Joe Canyon, which enters from the left. There's a mine up the tributary canyon. An old grader and other machinery are out by the river. A rough road goes several miles down the left bank, where maps show it connecting with a route out Spring Canyon.

Once out of the tight meanders and out of the Wingate Sandstone, the walls tend to be much less sheer, much more broken. There are spires, ledges, fallen blocks, and many small reentrants going back into the rock. Much of this is on the left, for some reason.

Not all tributaries are long and deep. Some are mere alcoves, perhaps with a small grove of cottonwoods and a water seep to support them. Occasionally, a talus slope comes down from such an alcove and has brought large boulders to the river.

74.8 Cairn that somebody built of stones, on the right. There will be more of these as you float around Spring Canyon Point.

73.2 An old inscription, "Launch Marguerite," is visible from the river, on the face of a rock.

The river still sweeps around curves in this stretch, but the curves are not so tight and regular. You will soon be turning left around Spring Canyon Point.

71.8, **71.6** and **71.3** Three small canyons come down to the river. The second and third have nice camps. The first appears to have a camp also, though I didn't look soon enough to be sure. Satellite photos at maps.google.com seem to show a camp—so I marked it in yellow.

We almost camped at the last of these in 2004, but wanted to make a few more miles. A consideration: You can't see from here to know if the camp at the neck of Bowknot Bend is occupied and it's far to the next camp thereafter. This is reason to keep track of other parties on the river, and talk with them about where they'll be going that night.

69.6 Camp (38°36.50'N 110°01.56'W) from which you can walk over the ridge at Bowknot Bend. The route appears to climb on or near some orange-colored talus. "Wimmer," a historic name, is painted on a large rock near camp, and dated "1/09." "Marguerite" is on another rock.

The river draws close to itself here before swinging seven miles around Bowknot Bend. The ridge is sharp because it's been eroded from both sides. From just past mile 70 you can walk steeply up and over. There's a "river register" on top with names on slabs of rocks. The BLM has asked that river people not add new names to it.

67.5 Mouth of Spring Canyon. I know there's a camp in there, but you're not going to get to it except when the river is quite high.

Green River to Mineral Bottom 15

The name "Wimmer" on a rock near the camp at mile 69.6, carrying a date of January, 1909

At very high water we once floated inflatable kayaks in via the mouth of the tributary. But at 7K we could only float about 100 yards up the crooked wash, and we found no opening through the tammies.

66.6 Camp on an island, at lower water.

66.3 Wide sandbar camp on the right, at lower water.

62.4 The BLM has inventoried a camp at Oak Bottom, though I haven't looked for myself. There would be a steep carry up the bank. The trail over the neck of Bowknot Bend descends near here.

61.4 Nice camp with another steep carry. There's a good view up the river and somebody has placed flat rocks to sit on. Was this one of several steamboat stops in the old days? A trail goes a few tens of yards upstream, and then turns a corner into the wash.

61.0 Camp on the left—and just downstream, a camp on the right.

60.8 Mouth of Twomile Canyon.

59.4 Mouth of Horseshoe Canyon. This, together with another canyon just above, makes an expansive opening in the canyon wall. It's a rincon around which the river used to flow. Since being cut off, the river has cut deeper so that the rincon is "perched." The two limbs are now tributaries to the Green. A mass of rock stands centrally between them at the rincon's center, and its nose appears to point at you.

58.3 Possible camp on the left.

56.2 Mouth of Hell Roaring Canyon.

52.2 There's a long approach past Mineral Bottom to the takeout on the left. A dirt ramp slopes down to the river through a break in the tamarisk. A small brown sign names the place.

Don't worry if you don't see the ramp for a while. It's well down the bottom where the river begins to turn. This said, don't miss the takeout! The next is about 100 miles downstream through Stillwater Canyon, past the confluence with the Colorado River and then through Cataract Canyon.

There's another way: By prearrangement, a jet boat can meet you at the confluence and take you up the Colorado to Moab. Labyrinth and Stillwater Canyons are both popular canoe trips. See *River Access*.

The river keeps on flowing. It rounds a curve and will soon enter Stillwater Canyon. New rocks will rise above the water, among them the prominent White Rim Sandstone which forms a canyon rim in Stillwater. The White Rim Trail for 4WD and mountain bicycles runs atop that rim all the way around Canyonlands onto the Colorado River side.

At the bottom of its abyss, the water flows calmly. After 52 miles, the confluence appears suddenly. Yet another chapter begins in the story of this remarkable river, beyond the ones you just experienced.

Spires of Wingate Sandstone below Bowknot Bend

Above-right, Crystal Geyser in eruption

Above-left and below, deposion of crystaline material in the wet area near Crystal Geyser

Pool in Three Canyon, at very low water in 2004

*Above, late afternoon sun from our camp at mile 87.3
Below, last light across the river from the same camp*

The river up against the Wingate Sandstone, Labyrinth Canyon

River Access

Common Labyrinth Canyon launch areas are Green River State Park, Crystal Geyser, and Ruby Ranch. The takeout is at Mineral Bottom, 68 river miles below Green River, Utah.

The required river permit can be obtained at river access points, and at several other places such as the John Wesley Powell River History Museum at the east end of Green River. You fill out the form, take a copy on the river with you, and leave the other copy in the box where you got it. You can download a form from the BLM website and two copies will print. Just leave the "agency copy" in the box at your launch site and take the other with you. For the URL and phone, see *Introduction*.

Your trip may be checked to see if you have the required equipment—a portable toilet and firepan in particular. I just take (and use) what I generally must take on rivers. Much information is available from the Bureau of Land Management at the URL above, or by phone.

Green River State Park, river-right, mile 120

A well-used launch for Labyrinth Canyon is Green River State Park, right in the town of Green River, Utah. Take either of the two Green River exits from Interstate 70: Exit 164 from the east or 160 from the west. You'll end up on the main street of town. I-70 evidently stretched: not long ago, mile markers and exit numbers along here were all increased by two.

Note: Exits and mileposts along interstate highways are numbered in miles from the western or southern border of most states. But I-70 begins at I-15 halfway across Utah, and the numbers begin there.

Toward the east end of town, but still west of the river bridge and the West Winds Truck Stop, find a small sign on the south side of the street that says "Green River State Park." Turn south.

The street you've turned onto will curve around to the left because it follows a long-abandoned river meander. Turn into Green River State Park and pay at the booth. If it's late and you owe money, a ranger will be around in the morning to correct that situation.

Almost ready at Green River State Park

You can also turn south on Long Street. You'll come to another street that curves around the southern margin of the town. Turn east there and follow that road around to the state park entrance.

If you feel more adventurous and have time, turn south across the train tracks near the south end of town. You'll be headed toward the Green River airport. Partway there, the Green River Road angles off to the left. This is the route to some spectacular overlooks from the rim of Labyrinth Canyon if you know just where to go. It really helps to have gone to the Powell Museum for a copy of *The Labyrinth Rims* by Jack Bickers. I have it, and it's still hard to find some of the turns.

As you drive in through the state park gate, the river launch area is ahead and to your left. Camping is ahead and to your right. It's a beautiful, well kept, grassy camping area with trees. The state park will add to your Labyrinth Canyon trip experience.

If your vehicle is being shuttled, you'll be able to leave it near the launch area. There's parking. You may have to detach your trailer, so make sure your shuttle service knows to hook it up again, as well as which one to take.

The park fee is $14 to camp, which includes a free launch. Launching only is $5. If your vehicle will remain there more than a day, there's an additional daily fee. The park phone number is 435-564-3633.

The aforementioned John Wesley Powell River History Museum in Green River is well worth a visit. It's at the northeast corner of the bridge over the river. Across the road from there is the Tamarisk, a restaurant overlooking the river. Ray's Tavern downtown is a mecca for river people. Ben's serves both Mexican and American food. There's a restaurant beside the truck stop, and fast food near motels to the east.

Crystal Geyser, river-left, mile 115.2

To reach Crystal Geyser from Green River, drive east out of town, and cross the river. Go until you cross Interstate 70 at exit 164. Or turn off I-70 there, if that's your situation. Find the frontage road along the south side of I-70 and go east. There will be a right turn after 2.2 miles onto a dirt road that's smoother than the paved one you just left. Crystal Geyser is 6.2 miles from I-70. There's another right turn very near the end.

Some like this launch, though getting there may be more trouble than floating the five miles of river from the state park. Plus, you'll miss those thundering riffles down by the railroad trestle!

Crystal Geyser can be a good alternative for trips where a driver is going to drop you off, leave, and pick you up at the end—or where your car is going to be shuttled that same day. Be aware that this place may sometimes become a party-site at night.

Ruby Ranch, river-left, mile 97

This is a good launch, and saves 23 miles at the start of your trip. The ramp is opposite the mouth of the San Rafael River, about five miles above the beginning of Labyrinth Canyon. Ruby Launches make much sense.

River Access   23

To get there, take exit 175 from I-70. This is east of Green River but short of exit 182—which is Crescent Junction where Highway 191 from Moab joins I-70.

Drive south on a good dirt road for about 16 miles, going through two gates near the end. The rule about gates is to leave them as you found them! Generally, that means you will close them again, and you ought not fail. NOTE: THESE GATES WILL BE LOCKED ON SUNDAYS, AND YOU CANNOT REACH RUBY RANCH ON THAT DAY.

Immediately after the second gate, you will be facing a large, oval field that occupies a river bottom. Across the field you will see cottonwood trees that line the river. You'll drive down to the field and turn right around its edge. Continue around the field, and you'll arrive between some corrals and a ranch house. A new house is being built on a hill to the south.

You'll see a sign about launch and camping fees. It's $10 per boat and $2 per person to launch. If you camp, that

Ranger Alan Jackson, a fixture at the Mineral Bottom access

costs another $2 per person. Put your money in the box below the sign. Also in the box is a loose-leaf notebook containing Bureau of Land Management permit applications. Fill one out, leave one copy in the book, and take the other copy down the river with you. These are picked up periodically by BLM personnel.

Just past the box, turn left across a ditch and through the fields. You'll come to a place where the road may be muddy. Chris, owner of Atomic Shuttle in Moab, certainly confirmed the existence of this mud and has her own special name for the place. It was really muddy when I first went in there. But next time, it was dry.

Launch and camping area at Ruby Ranch

You'll come to a shady area with large trees and a good (though not wide) ramp down to the river. There's a large wooden wire spool that serves as a table. You'll see an old kayak of unknown origin.

When I checked out Ruby Ranch in 2004, I met co-owner Kerry Rozman, who told me that they do other things besides allow boat launches. They have a cabin about a mile upstream, and are open for various kinds of gatherings, reunions, or other. There are inner tubes available so that guests who wish to can float along the Ranch's three miles of river frontage. Ranch e-mail is therubyranch@starband.net and the phone is 435-650-3193.

Mineral Bottom, river-left, mile 52

The take-out at Mineral Bottom is reached from Green River by driving east on I-70 to exit 182, then going toward Moab on Highway 191 for around 20 miles. Alter these directions as needed for your direction of travel. Turn toward Canyonlands National Park on Utah 313 and go not quite to the border of the park. Turn right onto the road to Mineral Bottom, which is marked by a small sign before the Dead Horse Point/Canyonlands junction. It's then 17 miles to Mineral Bottom. This dirt road crosses relatively flat terrain until it reaches the rim of the canyon.

Then the road plunges dramatically over the edge and switchbacks spectacularly down the face of a Navajo and Wingate Sandstone cliff. At the bottom, you'll see the western terminus of the White Rim Trail. Continue upriver and arrive at the Mineral Bottom river access area.

A canoe trip bound for the confluence, stopped with Ranger Alan at Mineral Bottom for Canyonlands National Park ~~permit~~ purposes

This ramp was made by miners during the uranium boom in the fifties. There's plenty of parking, and room to camp if that's your plan. The river ranger lives in a small trailer.

Shuttle services will leave your car just upstream in another parking area, and an airstrip is upstream of that. Artifacts (dead vehicles) from former mineral exploration days can be seen in the area.

Safety of Vehicles

Ruby Ranch seems safer for vehicles than any other river access area I know about. Green River State Park and Mineral Bottom both seem safe, particularly given the remoteness of the latter. But since Crystal Geyser can be a party site, I hold doubts about that area.

Shuttle, Aircraft, and Jet Boat Services

Updated in 2005 from the shuttle services listed on the BLM site. They are in alphabetical order by category:

Vehicle Shuttle Services:

Atomic Shuttle, Moab 435-259-6475, ckauhi@preciscom.net

Green River Shuttle Service, Green River 435-564-8292

Mary's Shuttle Service, Green River 435-564-8381

Red River Canoe Company, Moab 435-259-7722

River Runners Shuttle Service, Green River 800-241-2591, 435-259-3512 toll free, 435-260-2019, www.desertsw.com

Trent and Kaycee Fluckey, Green River 877-597-5479, 435-564-8383 toll free, www.greenriveraviation.com

Air Services:

(To/from the strip at Mineral Bottom, or other services)

Green River Aviation (Trent Fluckey), 877-597-5479 toll free, www.greenriveraviation.com

Redtail Aviation 435-259-7421

Slickrock Air Guides 435-259-6216

Jet Boat Services:

(from the confluence, if you're going on)

Tag-A-Long, Moab 800-453-3292

Tex's River Ways, Moab 435-259-5101

The Horsethief Trail spectacularly climbs the cliff from Mineral Bottom

Four Labyrinth Trips

Aerial Recon

It was January of 1967. A friend and I flew Labyrinth, Stillwater, and Cataract Canyons during our college years. Scott and I landed at Moab but the price of transportation into town made us jump back into my dad's Stinson for the short flight over to Green River. That airport was then located on the west edge of town and dinner was a quick walk away. Californians then, we had just discovered winter but the airport operator let us use our sleeping bags in the terminal that night.

We flew down the Green River in the morning. I didn't know such names as Little Valley, Three Canyon, Ten Mile Bottom, or even Labyrinth. But these rivers fascinated me, as they do now.

I'd never personally seen a river boat, and there weren't many then. But I owned *Time and the River Flowing,* the Sierra Club's new volume that described and illustrated a boat trip through the Grand Canyon. That book helped rally the nation against dams there, and it would help me become a river person.

What's around that next bend? Many folks look at rivers and wonder that. This particular river was frozen over at the time, and I remember a long strip of white that curved among the red cliffs and buttes. I liked discovering what was around those bends and I still do.

When I flew an airplane for a chain of Colorado mortuaries one year, uncomplaining passengers didn't seem to mind if I banked steeply to make a photograph over the rivers of Canyon Country. Later, still living in central Colorado, my own Piper Tripacer would provide wings of exploration.

After this, rowing rafts down those same rivers felt like an up-close continuation of an ongoing thing. I just got wet more often.

1984

An initial exploration of Labyrinth Canyon was in order. The water was very high that June—about 30,000 cubic feet per second. This would be a simple flatwater trip, so we'd do it in a simple way. We took two inflatable kayaks. I had no clue that I'd ever be writing about it.

Toni and I left our kayaks and gear with Glen Baxter, the now-retired operator of Redtail Aviation at the Green River airport. He'd flown other shuttles for us. We drove to Mineral Bottom, 68 miles down the Green River from town, and camped. See *River Access.*

At the appointed hour in the morning, Glen landed at the strip that's just upstream of the Mineral Bottom river access. Levitation up out of the canyon was quick, and the flight back to the Green River airport was short. Then Glen drove us over to Green River State Park to launch.

Calm river near Little Valley

We made good time that first day, as happens at high water. After a stop at Crystal Geyser, we flushed on past Little Valley, Ruby Ranch, and the mouth of the San Rafael to camp on the right at Bull Bottom, mile 93.

An opening through the tamarisk was obvious then, but vegetation grows, and it isn't open anymore. It was just below a trail that clings to the sandstone face and slopes downstream to the bottomland. Since then, I've driven from Green River to the top of this trail.

In the morning, we made the quick float to Three Canyon on Trin Alcove Bend, mile 90. At 30,000 cfs we were able to paddle the inflatable kayaks about 200 yards up the wash to a wonderful and seldom-used camp under large trees.

Our camp was near the confluence of two canyons (Powell said three but I'd say two plus a small one) that join and go together out to the river. At more ordinary water levels you can't float up into this wash at all. People usually don't camp where we did, so we felt privileged in our beautiful place. There were other Navajo Sandstone canyons like this one, but Powell Reservoir destroyed them.

Not particularly early in the morning, we floated on. Below Three Canyon, the Green follows a groove that meanders tightly, back and forth, traversing the Glen Canyon Group of sandstones. Between river miles 84 and 77 the river advances by three straight-line miles—not seven.

Imagine a centerline drawn downstream through the system of meanders: The canyon takes six fairly symmetrical excursions about that line. In each of these, the river flows straight for the better part of a mile, deeply entrenched in Labyrinth Canyon now. Then it rounds a big curve against a wall of Wingate Sandstone and glides back in nearly the opposite direction, roughly half a mile from its former self. On a map, it looks as though a snake has folded itself tightly and flat along the bottom of a straight passageway that's about three times wider than the snake itself.

A little beyond these tight meanders is Bowknot Bend, where the Green loops eastward. It's only a quarter mile from river mile 70 across the neck of the bend to mile 63. But to get there, the river flows seven miles.

Along the eastern side of this big excursion, we floated the kayaks up the wash at Spring Canyon (as we'd done at Three Canyon) and camped. The float out to Mineral Bottom in the morning was quick.

2001

Great plans can go awry! This would not be our finest river trip.

Seventeen years had passed. On 9 June 2001 Jeanette and I launched my cataraft from Green River State Park. This time I knew I'd be writing about it, and I was there to make notes and photographs. I took two cameras and intended to spend time getting to know the place much better.

Many canoe trips come this way. Indeed, while flying the river I'd noticed a row of canoes beached at the mouth of Three Canyon. Having spoken with canoeists, I knew they needed a guide and map to this section of river. My cataraft had been down much whitewater, from the Arkansas near home to the Grand Canyon. But now, we accepted Labyrinth's flatwater because the canyon was wild and beautiful.

We camped at the beautifully wooded Green River State Park, and floated away in the morning. I'd expected much higher water in early June, but the river was only flowing about 8,000 cfs—around half my prediction and just over a quarter of what we'd had that first time.

But Jeanette and I were off—first under the railroad bridge at Green River and then under Interstate 70. Several little riffles were there, around islands and at the highway bridge. We didn't realize how good a riffle would seem by the time we took out.

We walked around at Crystal Geyser on the orange, wet, rippled rock being deposited there by the mineralized water. Picnickers were about.

Very early, it looked as though a canyon was developing. But that was just a tease. The canyon teases the boater again down through The Auger, a small rapid just past Crystal Geyser. It looked like we were floating into wild country, though we weren't. The cliffs rose tantalizingly, but quickly fell away again.

Past The Auger and the cliffs, we noticed an ongoing ranch operation in Little Valley, a large bottomland on the left. A few old cabins were visible from the water. The river flows westward here, and the jagged flank of the San Rafael Swell is seen several miles ahead. We rounded a curve to the left against a gray wall of Mancos Shale that might have signaled a terrain change, but didn't.

Most land along here is private. At Nine Mile Wash (which is less than a mile from Five Mile Wash) there's an old cabin. Roads of unknown condition reach the right side of the river here. Access to this area, and to the west rim of Labyrinth Canyon, is via the Green River Road which goes south from the town.

Decrepit old waterwheels are seen on the left side in this vicinity. Innovatively, one is not straight up and down but has its axle at an angle to the horizontal so that the wheel reaches out to the water. Another waterwheel never performed its intended work because it was built in an eddy. Oops! Maybe there's more to this story, like a shift in the river channel. I hope so, but I don't know.

Again, it appeared that a canyon was developing. On we floated among some hills, over the Salt Wash Graben, and past Salt Wash itself. We stopped for a bit at a camp near the upstream end of Anvil Bottom, above which stands Dellenbaugh's Butte. This prominence was named by Powell after the young artist on his 1871 river trip, and also bears the local names Anvil and Inkwell. It was a fine camp, but we wanted to float farther.

The San Rafael River entered the Green through a narrow opening in the tamarisk, as streams in the southwest tend to do. I've not done this, but you can kayak down the San Rafael for about 25 miles and emerge here, given that there's enough water in the small tributary. The access at Ruby Ranch should be accessible, directly across the Green.

Water pumps on Ruby Ranch were being driven by loud engines, the necessity of which I understood. We floated just past the noise, and camped on the right. Camps were not numerous in this stretch, and we were afraid to pass this one up.

The water had recently and quickly dropped to around 8,000 cfs from 13,000 and the banks were mostly muddy: so muddy where we camped, and so steep, that we didn't even unload our cooking equipment. Rather, we made do with food that didn't require heat. Fortunately, I was in the company of a food-genius and we ate well.

In the morning (not having to load so much stuff at least means you get off earlier) we reached Three Canyon at mile 90. Jeanette and I beached the cataraft at the mouth of the wash and walked up to a bench on the upstream side of the tributary canyon. What a great camp this would be! Set against a steep wall that actually overhangs a bit, it would be sufficient for larger groups.

Back to the river we went, and on to a camp at mile 84. There are a number of long-established camps in Labyrinth, and this was one of them. It had a nice landing and a flat cooking area near the boat. Up a bank was a grove of trees where we pitched our tent. Our steaks were earned and excellent.

On the rock wall behind camp were the names of some early river travelers. People have been floating this section of the Green for a while now, at first for reasons unrelated to water sports. Some were ranchers, prospectors, trappers—or even early steamboaters.

Having fun was surely not the boaters' purpose. The river enterprises mostly failed, but I wonder if they found satisfaction here? I don't know. That some of them painted their names on rocks may indicate an awareness that being on the river was extraordinary.

Camp at mile 84

They didn't just go *down* the river: imagine, if you can, these people rowing heavy boats *up* the Green! Some left Moab on the Colorado River, floated to the confluence, and then traveled upstream to Blake (present-day Green River). Hearing train whistles meant they were almost there at last. This confounds the mind, as do many of their strenuous deeds.

Some of the names on the rock behind this camp were likely those of pioneering river people. I recognized the name of one old-time rancher, and the date "1909" was there.

So, what was wrong with this trip? How did it go awry? Until then, it had been fine. But as soon as we went up into the trees to pitch our tent, we were dived upon by buzzing hordes of mosquitoes.

Repellent helped only a little. After getting the tent up and our camp secured for the night, there was nothing we could do but zip in and go to bed. Mosquitoes that had gotten inside the tent were severely dealt with. But because of the ones outside there would be no sitting by the river until dark reading, talking, writing notes, walking about to photograph, or anything else. Our tent was our prison.

Morning came, and the mosquito situation was no better. It wasn't quite as bad down by the water, though we still felt inspired to hurry. We didn't even cook breakfast. I had intended to photograph some of the names on the rock, but I didn't. In a spirit of great urgency, we packed our gear, loaded it on the boat, and were off down the river just before seven.

Once out on the water, there were no bugs. Food came from our large supply of snacks. Fig bars make a wonderful river breakfast in time of need.

Huge fish swam along very near the surface and seemed interested in sucking down the foam that forms on rivers: I'd never seen them before. The foam must contain nutrients, though we humans would not consider it tasty. We'd see a disturbance in the water, reminiscent of a submarine shallowly gliding along. There'd be similar disturbances elsewhere. Sometimes the ripples seemed to come toward the boat, but if one got too near an oar there'd be a quick splash and the large creature would vanish into deepness.

A wild turkey youngster on the shore was being soundly scolded by a parent, who apparently thought it foolhardy to venture near the water as we passed.

Near mile 79, a group we'd seen the previous afternoon was spread out downstream among the trees. Not everyone had been driven out of camp as we had been.

In this area, gnats were even thicker than mosquitoes had been at our camp—but they didn't bite. Seen against a shadowed rocky wall in morning light, they looked like mist.

We passed through Labyrinth's series of tight meanders after our hurried departure. These made for good floating because the magnificent scenery would change each mile or so.

Just beyond the meanders, there's an inscription on a rock about the Launch Marguerite, a boat that used to ply the river and which perhaps stopped there at mile 73. There were names on rocks, too. Remnants of a trail went along the right, and there were two cairns nearly a mile apart. Labyrinth Canyon's human history is very rich.

After coming over Bowknot Bend, the hiking route back to the river slopes downstream from the western end of the neck. Two boys were standing on a rock near Oak Bottom as we passed. They'd been dropped off, and said it had been a good walk over. Their party was coming around on the river and would camp there.

They had hand-held two way radios—the low powered kind sold for personal communication—but of course these were useless around bends in the canyon. I hope they didn't drain their batteries trying.

We floated on and camped above Twomile Canyon (spelled this way on the USGS map). The carry up was steep though the boat landing was fine. A trail went over into and turned up a large drainage. The view farther upstream was to the termination of Bowknot Bend.

Mosquitoes were as before, so again we didn't cook. We just set up the tent, snacked, and crashed. We escaped the bloodsucking little insects and that's almost all we did. There were old names on the wall here, too, but I didn't photograph them as I normally would have.

Jeanette and I discussed the function of bats in the ecosystem. Where were the bats, our potential saviors? In the Grand Canyon, we hadn't seen mosquito one, but bats fluttered around our camps right after dark. The correlation is definite. In Labyrinth we saw no bats. Maybe they require proper habitat and it wasn't there. Biodiversity is a wonderful thing, as certain of our leaders (I write in 2005) don't appear to fathom.

In the morning we packed up quickly and got on the water early. The character of the canyon changed as we floated downstream from Twomile Wash. The walls got craggier and more complex. From Mineral Bottom, up and out of the canyon we went, to a good meal in Moab. That meal did not include pita pockets, cookies, or fig bars.

There may be things that you're glad to have endured but wouldn't want to experience in quite the same way again. This trip was among them. Instead, how would a perfect and beautiful Labyrinth trip be?

2004

In June of 2004, with a new boat and a different companion, it was time for another Labyrinth trip. With a river guide rough draft at hand, we stoically launched. No waiting for later in the season—there was work to be done, photographs to be made, and maps to be checked. Tough work, this, but how else would it happen?

After discussion of the last trip's difficulties, Sandra and I each bought pullover mosquito netting for our heads, and packed lots of DEET-rich repellent. So armed, we prepared our minds and souls for the coming battle with bugs.

For the duration of *this* trip I think we saw three mosquitoes—and they were timid! So where was the buzzing horde of bugs, that bloodthirsty fog? Mosquito netting went to the bottom of our bags. I think we applied repellent at first, just on principle, but it wasn't necessary. We slept under the stars each night, not in a tent. There was no rain, and very little wind. There were probably a couple dozen harmless little gnats. It was the sought-after perfect trip.

Ruby Ranch was our launch. This cut 23 miles off the trip: miles that are comparatively uninspirational. Ruby is at mile 97, about 5 miles above the beginning of Labyrinth Canyon.

We picked up Chris, of Atomic Shuttle, in Moab. We all had dinner together and then headed for Ruby Ranch. We unloaded the boat and the equipment as Chris assured us that she'd never known anyone to leave anything they needed. I saw my tail lights move off across the ranch, stop while Chris opened and closed the gate, then go up the hill toward Moab and finally Mineral Bottom. It was a done deal.

Chris likes to do shuttles in this way because she doesn't have to hire a driver and make a special trip out to the launch to pick up the vehicle. She knows that the key works (which hasn't always been the case) and she knows how much gasoline is in the tank.

Register Rock, atop the talus left of center

Ruby Ranch was a fine launch with a good camp, if you neglect the loud pumps that must run to water the fields. In the morning it was just seven miles to Three Canyon instead of thirty, so we were able to explore there and still float down the river that same day.

Sandra and I had just talked about spending half an hour apart each day, to do our own things. She sat down beside the river to read, and I headed up the canyon. But I was gone nearly two hours! Curiosity and cameras are very dangerous in that way.

This time I saw a way to walk up the canyon with wet, but not muddy, feet. I'd been told there was a fine spring pool up there so I followed the small stream of water. I'm not sure whether I found the acclaimed spring, but I did come to a place where the canyon was undercut on the south-most side and a shallow pool existed. I suspect this was it, and that continued drought had lowered the water.

About a hundred yards down the river, Sandra remembered something left on the beach. We landed, and she started back up to get it, soon disappearing into the tamarisk jungle that covers the bottom of Three Canyon out near the river. I could track her progress by noticing where the greenery was moving. But that soon stopped. Sandra, I'd learn later, was by then snaking laboriously through the thickness on hands and knees.

I saw her emerge from the tamarisk about halfway back to the beach and enter the river. She then swam upstream, even around a small point that deflected a jet of water. She picked up what had been left (waterproof binoculars), reentered the water, and swam easily back to the raft. Sandra is a very strong swimmer, whereas nobody is a good tamarisk crasher.

We floated almost three more miles down to a good camp on the left. There, we devoured steaks and went for a short walk up the small canyon behind the camp. It was quite steep, and I was too tired to trust myself on the large boulders. Sandra climbed higher than I did, and found columbine growing where water seeps out between layers of rock.

Head of tributary canyon at mile 84

Upstream, we saw a canoe group obviously looking for a camp. They'd walk around, then canoe down farther. Even before they arrived, we'd talked and had decided to share our spacious camp.

One of these students from Utah Valley State College had just participated in the now-infamous April canoe race down the Green River from Crystal Geyser to Mineral Bottom. Usually it's a fun event, but in 2004 the challenges were much more severe than normal.

Wind and cold happened. Jeremy told us about 50 mph gusts of wind that day. Participants were often not dressed for such extremes— there were girls wearing bikinis and flip-flops in the cold. Many had never been on a river before.

Canoes at mile 84

Cactus upstream of Bull Bottom

Straight sections of river developed three-foot swells. Bureau of Land Management personnel were out most of the night rescuing people who ended up shivering in tents, lying spoon-style to conserve warmth. For many, it was a rather uncomfortable time. But against the predictions of some, I hope this event will resume in the future.

On down the tight meanders we went. After investigating several camps for writing purposes, we floated to the one near mile 70, very near the upstream side of the neck where Bowknot Bend begins.

We'd been joking about "river Nazis." For example, the cooler Nazi is the enemy of heat transfer and counts off seconds whenever the cooler lid is open. The recycling Nazi watches for violations of what most of us quietly practice anyway. Various other types, such as the propane Nazi, can be identified. Personally, I am most of these rolled into one, but I try to be nice about it.

At this last camp, on the opposite canyon wall by evening's light and shadows, was the image of a bellowing Nazi. You can try and find him if you're there, but you'll probably have a better trip if you fail.

Regional Geology

Sandstone walls tower over you. Some are nearly vertical, and their color ranges from white, to brown, to red. Though you started in open country, you're in Labyrinth Canyon now, floating down a river whose deep canyon winds back and forth. How did this all come to be? Why is this river canyon so spectacular?

The rock around you got there grain by grain, and it's going down the river the same way. But isn't that true everywhere? Why is this place so very special? A fortunate sequence of events happened here.

Precambrian rock is far below, and you won't see any on this trip. The Precambrian Era comprised about 70% of geologic time, from the formation of the earth until about 570 million years ago.

The Precambrian "basement" rocks are, by definition, crystalline. New minerals were often formed from the constituents of older ones by metamorphism under great heat and pressure. Telltale signs often lie in the arrangement of crystals, as well as in the minerals formed. These metamorphics, themselves quite hot, were often penetrated by igneous material that solidified into masses of granite upon cooling. Much more happened then, but that's not our subject here.

Above the Precambrian basement are the Paleozoic rocks. They're mostly sediments—some were deposited on the bottoms of the shallow seas that repeatedly intruded. If you continue past Mineral Bottom as many trips do, headed either for Cataract Canyon or to the confluence for a jet boat shuttle to Moab, you'll encounter Paleozoic rocks as you continue to move "downsection." That means deeper into the rock, and farther back in time.

The sedimentary rock layers are thousands of feet higher at your takeout than at your launch. That is why floating downstream takes you deeper into the canyon. Older and older rocks are exposed down-canyon because the sedimentary layers "dip" to the north. That is, they're tilted in that direction. A basketball, placed on an exposed bedding surface here, would roll north.

The river enters the Uinta Basin from Split Mountain, at the end of a Lodore trip. How the Canyon of Lodore was cut through the Uinta range, and the development of Desolation and Gray Canyons, are stories for another time. See *Desolation and Gray Canyons River Guide.*

This sequence of older and older rocks begins about 100 straight-line miles north of your Labyrinth launch, above Desolation and Gray Canyons. It begins where the Green River leaves the Uinta Basin, and ends in the Paleozoic rocks of Cataract Canyon.

Although the Green enters Mesozoic rock upstream near the head of Gray Canyon, Labyrinth Canyon is a tour through most of the Mesozoic section. These rocks have been there since the time of dinosaurs. This era

Mancos Shale across from Little Valley

of geologic time was between about 245 and 66 million years ago.

About 75 million years ago, there lived a small mammal among the big reptiles. These little guys never dreamt of calculus, literature, world travel, river boats, or geology. But they were our ancestors and the common ancestors of every other mammal on the earth today.

In late Mesozoic time, a sea intruded into this region from the east, then withdrew as lands first began to rise toward their present configuration. From this sea, the Mancos Shale was deposited—and gave us a classic example of the intrusion and withdrawal of a sea.

Consider where the launch is at Green River: It's in a broad valley through which highways and railroads can run. If you look north from there, you'll see the Book Cliffs from which Gray Canyon emerges.

Why is there a broad valley here at Green River instead of a river canyon? Well, the Mancos Shale is soft so it's a valley-former, not a cliff-former. Certain sandstones downstream are cliff-formers, to say the least! Where the shale rises to the surface in the tilted sequence of rocks, erosion has made it into a valley.

The Book Cliffs are largely of Mancos Shale, which is a rather drab, gray siltstone. What's this? The valley-forming Mancos makes up a cliff? Harder layers near the top of the Book Cliffs are slowing erosion of the soft, underlying Mancos—"holding it up," so to speak.

If you were rigging your boat at the site of Green River a million years ago, the Book Cliffs would have been nearer. In the future, the cliffs will have receded—and Gray Canyon will be shorter. That brown color in the river? It's upstream rock traveling seaward.

The Mancos is much coarser in the west, and finer grained to the east. Since fine sediment travels farther, the source area lay to the west. A problem has been this: What source area had been large enough to shed such a huge volume of sediment?

Look south from the town of Green River. Relatively open country is interspersed with hills and short canyons between Green River and the entrance into Labyrinth Canyon. This is because the river cuts through rock formations of varying characteristics in this tilted sequence. Also, parts of that sequence have been faulted up or down.

Very soon after you float under the railroad bridge near the launch, you'll pass through the Dakota Sandstone. This was the beach sand along the advancing edge of the intruding sea—the sea from which the Mancos would eventually be deposited.

A half mile later in your journey back through Mesozoic time, you're in the Brushy Basin Member of the Morrison Formation. At mile 118.6 there's evidence on the left of a landslide, which is part of the geologic process down here.

After yet another half mile, the Salt Wash Member of the Morrison Formation appears. Deposition was as giant alluvial fans, to which streams brought sediment from the region of today's Grand Canyon.

The Morrison was deposited by streams flowing into and over a broad, mostly land-locked plain where plants grew and animals lived. There was an outlet somewhere, but no other connection with the sea. The Salt Wash Member was of great interest to uranium prospectors on the Colorado Plateau just after the middle of the 20th century.

The Morrison is likely the most-studied formation on earth. Not just for uranium, but also for dinosaur fossils. The quarry far upstream in Dinosaur National Monument is one site. The Cleveland-Lloyd Quarry about 40 miles northwest of your launch is another.

The quarries differ: the one in Dinosaur was a stream channel sandbar deposit, while Cleveland-Lloyd was a flood plain environment. The clay matrix at Cleveland-Lloyd is much softer and can be scraped away with a knife. No hammers or chisels are needed there. Even tiny bones are preserved in what was likely a watery bog, according to William Stokes in *Geology of Utah,* 1986.

The fossil records differ too; many carnivores were fossilized at Cleveland-Lloyd, while they are rare at Dinosaur National Monument.

At about mile 116, the Summerville Formation rises from the river, first on the right and then on the left. During the time preceding the Morrison, shallow seas would periodically encroach, and there were bordering tidal flats. On those, the Summerville was deposited.

Crystal Geyser at mile 115.3 is obvious by the orange deposits all around it. This comes from water that erupts from the old well casing there. See photographs elsewhere in this book.

The Little Grand Fault crosses the river just downstream of the geyser. Here, the southern side of the fault is downthrown about 1000 feet, according to Mutschler, *River Runners' Guide to Canyonlands National Park and Vicinity.*

Earlier, you left the Mancos Shale behind. But because of the fault you'll soon see it again in the gray bluffs at mile 112.5, across the river from Little Valley which is the broad river bottom on the left. You'll see exposures of Morrison and Cedar Mountain Formation at the lower end of Little Valley.

I've never been on the ground in Little Valley—there's a locked gate on the road and "no trespassing" signs along the river in places. This is ranching land.

Between miles 109.2 and 108.5 you'll cross the Salt Wash Graben, the term for an area that sank between two faults. This one only sank about 200 feet, according to Mutschler. The graben doesn't show up very well from the river, but its continuation to the northwest is obvious on a topo map.

By mile 108.3, you're again into the Salt Wash Member of the Morrison, and will be until mile 103. Mutschler points out something interesting; there are gravel-capped terraces on seven different levels, from 10 feet to 350 feet above the river. Gravels came from the Uinta Mountains (which the river crosses) and also from the White River area of Colorado.

While making these terraces, sometimes the river would have been cutting laterally so as to widen a terrace. At other times, the river was downcutting to a level where a new terrace would form.

From mile 105.5, you'll be floating through a complete section of the Summerville Formation, as you did above the fault. This starts at mile 103.9 where the Summerville is overlain by the Salt Wash Member of the Morrison, and underlain by the Curtis. These rocks were deposited in wet to marginally marine conditions. There are evaporites in the Curtis that indicate restricted access to the open sea.

Near mile 102, you'll float past some modern sand dunes, with a set of slightly older dunes underneath. On the left near mile 102, a nice camp is backed against Entrada Sandstone. You'll be seeing more of this rock at mile 100, where it forms a cliff. Before the shallow seas and mudflats arrived, this area was much drier. Entrada sands were blown by the wind.

Entrada Sandstone forms the river bank here. It also forms Delicate Arch and other highlights of Arches National Park, as well as the goblins of Goblin Valley. This rock will be exposed on the right down to the mouth of the San Rafael River.

Below the San Rafael, the Carmel Formation is exposed. This is another shallow marine, or tidal flat, deposit. At mile 100.9 several formations are exposed on the left in Dellenbaugh's Butte.

At Bull Bottom, mile 93, you are nearing the entrance to Labyrinth Canyon. The Navajo Sandstone has begun to rise over the river. Other rocks still overlie the Navajo, but you're gonna get there!

The Navajo Sandstone is atop the Glen Canyon Group—these are the major rocks of Labyrinth Canyon. They and the river have given you important reason for boating there.

In this group, the Navajo and Wingate Sandstones resulted from sand dune deserts. Between them is the thinner and ledgier Kayenta Formation that came from a brief wetter time. Geologists sometimes call this part of Utah "The Great Sand Pile," and you're floating into it.

The Mesozoic had begun with the Pacific Ocean extending just into present-day Utah from the northwest. A series of island-arcs lay from present-day central Nevada across Oregon. The land sloped gently away from what little was left of Colorado's Ancestral Rockies to the east.

Note that at this time, the earth's equator ran through Utah in a present-day north-south direction. The continents have moved around rather dramatically.

Back to the part of the Mesozoic where you are, in your journey: Utah was much different from when the era began. The Pacific coast was farther away now. As the North American continent drifted across the Pacific, it crashed into whatever islands and island-arcs it came to. Some lands were accreted, becoming part of the continent. Other lands were subducted underneath North America.

The Navajo Sandstone formed after western Utah had risen into the Mesocordilleran High. We don't know how high it was, according to Stokes. He points out that this uplift was so close in time to America's separation from Europe that a "cause and effect relationship is reasonable." Uplift culminated in the Sevier Orogeny, but was overwith later in Mesozoic time.

During its long tenure, the high ground did several things: It blocked moisture from the west so that desert conditions prevailed in southeast Utah. It also provided a source for rivers that carried sediment eastward from the high country. Later, when a series of shallow seaways (from which were deposited the rocks you floated through earlier) intruded, they had to come in around the northern end of the western Utah high ground.

Wingate Sandstone, Spring Canyon

There is disagreement about whether the Navajo Sandstone was formed in water or on land. There is evidence for both, though most believe that this area involved transport of material by wind. Water was certainly present in places. Rivers may have flowed from the high country into the sand and then disappeared, according to Stokes.

The earlier Wingate Sandstone is considered to consist of sand driven by the Mesozoic wind. Sediment came from the source area to the southwest.

The earliest part of Mesozoic time was when red sediments were deposited in great thickness, not just in Utah but worldwide. The color of red rocks most often comes from iron, whose minerals can be highly colored and where a little bit goes a long way. Some vertical rock faces in the region have been stained by other minerals that washed down over them. This can cause them to look red or black, when they really aren't. This is called desert varnish.

The canyon walls become tall when you reach the Navajo Sandstone. You're in Labyrinth Canyon now! You'll pass through the Kayenta Formation and then into the Wingate Sandstone as you reach the stretch of tight meanders with vertical cliffs. After Bowknot Bend, the canyon begins to open out. This is because you have reached the bottom of the Wingate.

Down here, red rocks will appear as a slope beneath the tall Wingate Sandstone cliff. The softer Chinle Shale is underneath. This rock is also seen in the Painted Desert of Arizona.

By the time you get to Mineral Bottom, the Wingate cliff is still there and you'll have to drive up the Horsethief Trail to get out. But now the Wingate stands back from the river and there is softer, slope-forming rock below it.

It is the Glen Canyon Group of sandstones (Navajo through Wingate) that make Labyrinth Canyon the place it is. These rocks, of course, made Glen Canyon the place it was. Three Canyon at mile 90 is said to be the last Navajo Sandstone canyon of its kind not destroyed by Powell Reservoir.

The redbeds below the Wingate formed on land, not in the sea. That said, southeastern Utah was a wetter place just before Navajo-Wingate days. These Chinle and Moenkopi Formations will be the last rocks you'll come to on a Labyrinth trip.

So, the rocks you've been seeing were deposited mostly on low plains or in deserts, though a few were sea bottoms. How did they get to their present elevations, and how did the topography arrive at its present configuration? How did a large river cut a magnificent canyon through them?

Just before the Cenozoic Era, starting about 65 millions years ago, the sea that had intruded into Utah from the east (depositing the Dakota Sandstone, Mancos Shale, and others) withdrew toward the east. Why? This was an early indication of coming events. Laramide Orogeny, the great uplift of early Cenozoic time in the western United States, was at hand.

Stokes notes "a definite eastward shifting of geologic events." By late Mesozoic time, there had already been uplift in Nevada. Then the Sevier Orogeny of western Utah formed the Mesocordilleran High.

Now Laramide Orogeny was coming. Uplift came to the entire western United States, and moved eastward as far as Colorado's Front Range. The end of the mountains there is sharp and definite.

This happened because the continent was moving westward. It collided with whatever small landmasses it came to, and it overrode undersea crust. New land was created, and existing land was uplifted. Still during Mesozoic, the igneous mass was emplaced that later became the Sierra Nevada Range of California.

Various Laramide uplifts appeared: the San Rafael Swell was one. Its jagged rim is clearly visible ahead to the west as you float past Little Valley. The Uinta Mountains are another Laramide uplift. They appeared rather quickly in the north, and have since been cut through by the Canyon of Lodore.

Another part of eastern Utah was downwarped to form a large basin, into which sediments flooded. Later, that basin became a large, shallow lake from which more sediments were deposited. But you're in the wrong place to see all that. The right place is Desolation Canyon, upstream.

You will see no igneous (formerly molten) rocks in Labyrinth Canyon. There are, however, several large igneous bodies in the region. These include the Henry Mountains west of Cataract, the La Sals near Moab, The Abajos near Monticello, and Navajo Mountain near Page.

These mountains are laccoliths. That is, they consist of rather complex igneous intrusions that buckled up the overlying sedimentary rocks, rather than intruding through them.

After the Mesozoic, there was regional compression of the earth's crust, which led to folding and formation of mountains that were possibly quite high. Then, after great and dramatic change in the movement of crustal plates, the area was stretched 60–100 miles, according to Stokes. Effects of stretching are best seen elsewhere, both east and west.

In latest Mesozoic, only the Uintas may have had surface expression. Other structures were there, but had been smoothed off and maybe covered with sediments. Unlike today, southeastern Utah was without much topography. Several large, shallow lakes developed, and the sediments of Desolation Canyon were deposited from one.

Later, after the Green River had made its way southward through the Uintas, it flowed southward across lands that were about to rise. When that happened, the river had no choice but to cut these canyons. During this time, the continental divide shifted eastward from Nevada into Colorado.

After a regional uplift of the entire western United States during the last several million years, the Green/Colorado river system became one of the most actively eroding streams in the world. Witness the canyons it has cut! Active erosion of the main stream also steepened the tributaries, so that their canyons grew longer and deeper. This regional uplift is directly responsible for the magnificent canyons we float through today on the Green and Colorado Rivers.

Many rivers on the Colorado Plateau (as the area is called) have formed spectacular incised meanders. The Goosenecks of the San Juan are a world-class example (and are plainly seen from a spectacular overlook). Labyrinth Canyon is right up there with the San Juan.

Rivers flowing on nearly flat ground will meander in great loops—as does today's Mississippi River. Meanders on such rivers stand to become incised if the land rises. Meanders also are not firmly fixed in place but can slowly migrate in a downstream direction because there is more erosion on the outsides of curves than on the insides.

Tenmile Canyon enters the Green

When there is regional uplift, the river is suddenly given the ability to cut deeper. After just a bit of cutting, the meanders are much more fixed in place. The shape of the meanders will remain, but the river may end up at the bottom of a deep canyon. Labyrinth Canyon below mile 91 is like this, and particularly the miles between 85 and 76.

There still can be downstream movement of the meanders. Hence, there can still be cut offs, such as the one at Twomile. Someday, though not this year or nèxt, Bowknot Bend may be cut off.

Don't think that the story is over! It isn't. The canyons have reached a spectacular stage, but everything you see here is going away. Barring intervention, erosion is rapid enough to carry away the entire, multi-state Colorado Plateau in twenty million years, making of it a flat plain a few feet above sea level. Our particular view of this river is truly a bookmark in time. The Green River has never looked like this before, and it will never be like this again.

Above, view northwest as the Green River rounds Anvil Bottom at mile 102. A small geyser can be seen right of bottom-center where there is a spot of blue Below, view southwest where the river enters Labyrinth Canyon near mile 92

*Above, view eastward to Labyrinth near the mouth of Keg Spring Canyon
Below, looking eastward along the narrow neck of Bowknot Bend*

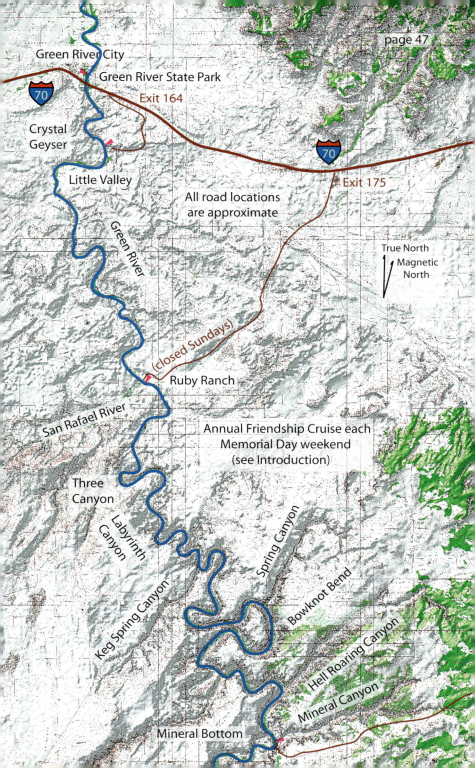

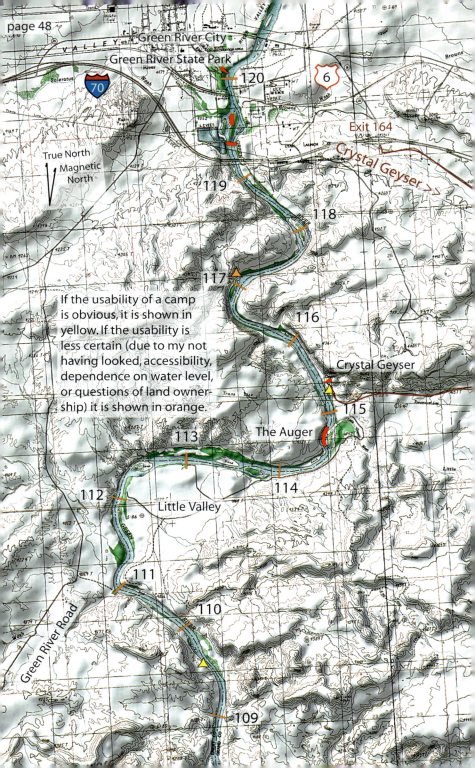

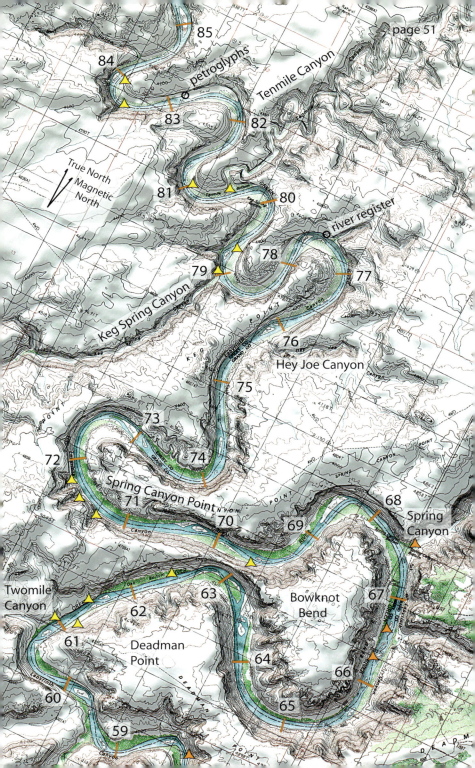